I0435103

Riparian Area Management

Riparian and Wetland
Classification

Review and Application

BLM

Technical Reference 1737-21
2005

by

Karl Gebhardt, P.E.
Hydrologist/Environmental Engineer
Bureau of Land Management
Boise, Idaho

Ervin Cowley
Natural Resource Specialist
Bureau of Land Management
Boise, Idaho

Don Prichard
Fishery Biologist/Riparian Coordinator
Bureau of Land Management
Denver, Colorado

Mike Stevenson
Hydrologist
Bureau of Land Management
Coeur d'Alene, Idaho

Suggested citations:

Gebhardt, K., D. Prichard, E. Crowley, and M. Stevenson. 2005. Riparian area management:
   Riparian and wetland classification review and application. Technical Reference 1737-21.
   U.S. Department of the Interior, Bureau of Land Management, Denver, CO.
   BLM/ST/ST-05/002+1737. 26 pp.

U.S. Department of the Interior. 2005. Riparian area management: Riparian and wetland
   classification review and application. Technical Reference 1737-21. Bureau of Land Management,
   Denver, CO. BLM/ST/ST-05/002+1737. 26 pp.

Acknowledgements

The authors wish to thank Steve Leonard and George Staidle, who authored Technical Reference 1737-5, *Riparian and Wetland Classification Review*, which provided the basis for this document. We also thank those who reviewed and commented on Technical Reference 1737-5: Paul Hansen, Bill Platts, Bud Kovalchik, Bob Wagner, Jim Fogg, Dan Muller, Mark Vinson, Allen Cooperrider, Ray Boyd, Allan Strobel, and Al Amen. In addition, we thank Tim Burton for his review of this document.

Table of Contents

I. Introduction

Since the release of Technical Reference (TR) 1737-5, *Riparian and Wetland Classification Review*, in 1990, the use of classification in riparian and wetland disciplines has been refined. Some of the previously described classification techniques have become increasingly popular, and new systems have emerged to fill the gaps identified by land managers, wetland regulators, and wetland scientists. While TR 1737-5 focused on vegetation classification methods, this Technical Reference presents a general discussion of several areas of classification related to riparian and wetland management and provides guidance on applying classification to solve land management problems.

There are a number of statements, questions, and theories that provide a context for using classification. Understanding these items is essential to the successful application of any classification system:

• *Classification should permit comparison and reproducibility, provide an estimate of potential success or failure, and improve communication.*

• *"…many salmon restoration projects fail because they rely on 'off-the-shelf' concepts and designs rather than developing site-specific understanding…" (Kondolf et al. 2003).*

• *Are we repeating the application of failed techniques because we are too lazy to monitor their effectiveness?*

• *"While both physical and biological criteria have been used to classify lotic system, successful integration of these related aspects into a single, process-based framework that encompasses a range of spatio-temporal scales remains a considerable challenge" (Thomson et al. 2004).*

• *"Classifying riparian vegetation therefore requires a full understanding of species distribution and succession, in relation to environmental parameters and disturbance factors over a large area" (Muller 1997).*

• *"Watershed and ecoregion frameworks are complementary. Watersheds provide the framework for determining the land/water associations, and ecoregions provide the framework for extrapolating and reporting this information" (Omernik 2003).*

• *As with any procedure, misapplication is likely to occur if the users rely solely on the classification tool or its products and not on the underlying science behind the classification. Users must always place the science in front of the classification and not the other way around.*

• *Riparian and wetland systems are dynamic. Mapping and classification often produce only a snapshot that does not represent the dynamics of the system.*

• *Conducting riparian and wetland projects without examining site history and process is irresponsible.*

• *Do we want the right answer or the easy answer?*

II. Purpose of Classification

Classification is defined as a systematic arrangement of items into groups or categories according to established criteria. The purpose of classification for land management applications often has to do with providing a reasonably easy way to talk about management areas, establish priorities for decisionmaking, determine cost-effective strategies for dealing with resource restoration, or simply provide a basis to summarize inventory data into meaningful groups. Kondolf (1995) states that "classification allows scientists to stratify an otherwise confusing universe into sets of similar objects, conduct careful study on representative objects, and apply results to other members of that class." Classification should permit comparison and reproducibility, provide an estimate of potential success or failure, and improve communication.

In TR 1737-5, a number of vegetation classification systems were described so that practitioners could choose those that appeared most applicable to their needs. In the 15 years since the release of TR 1737-5, riparian and wetland classification requirements have expanded to encompass a variety of needs, and a number of applications have emerged that can benefit from classification strategies. Those applications most important to specialists in the Bureau of Land Management (BLM) include: environmental analysis, proper functioning condition (PFC) analysis, resource restoration, habitat creation, and wetland mitigation. Generally these applications require either a stratification of data for management presentation and discussion purposes or a stratification of data with cause and effect analysis. In recent years, cause and effect analysis has become the principal reason for beginning a classification effort.

III. Applying Classification

Technical Reference 1737-5 presented a number of vegetation classification systems and clearly stated that:

"It is the policy of the Bureau of Land Management (BLM) to apply the Standard Ecological Site Description procedure patterned after the Soil Conservation Service (SCS) Range Site procedure and expanded by the BLM (USDA-SCS 1976, USDI-BLM 1990) to grazable woodland, native pasture, and riparian sites. However, other classification and description procedures exist and often must be used to make use of all available information or to coordinate between other agencies and institutions during riparian and wetland inventory."

In the current century, specialists need to move towards an even better understanding of the systems they are attempting to manage. Many of the vegetation classification systems previously reviewed embraced the ecological concepts of vegetation succession, and some recognized the need to incorporate the hydrogeomorphic (and other) processes that influence often rapid and severe changes to vegetation communities (Youngblood et al. 1985, Kovalchik 1987, Hansen et al. 1988, Hansen 1989, Szaro 1989, Kovalchik and Chitwood 1990, and Hansen et al. 1995).

Gurnell et al. (1994) compiled stream classification methodologies from literature over the last century and grouped them in terms of spatial units from small to large:

- Habitat units—relatively small
- Sections—several hundred meters in length
- Zones—a bit larger, where a river would be described in terms of 3 or 4 zones
- Regions—watersheds and subwatersheds
- River—the whole river system
- Ecoregion—implying more than one river system
- Hierarchical—representing systems that have a nested range of units

The "early period," from 1890 through 1969, had 34 classification methodologies identified in the open literature, and the "late period," from 1970 through 1989, had 30. River and section classification systems accounted for 74 percent in the early period and 17 percent in the late period, while the hierarchical methods totaled 3 percent in the early period and 33 percent in the late periods. Heritage et al. (2001) state, "The majority of the hierarchies are structured from the catchment scale downward on the basis that it is the catchment variables that control the dynamics and, hence, the morphology of the river (Van Deusen 1954)." They also point out that the top-down hierarchy employed by many classifications, which assumes that the watershed system above a subsystem forms the environment of the subsystem, may not be applicable in all situations and cites Mosely (1987) as suggesting it may be more useful to classify rivers by their components, resulting in a bottom-up hierarchy. Thomson et al. (2004) state "While both physical and biological criteria have been used to classify lotic systems, successful integration of these related aspects into a single, process-based framework that encompasses a range of spatio-temporal scales remains a considerable challenge."

What we can conclude from the discussion above is that no single classification approach may be the best in every situation. We can, however, make some educated guesses at which system or combination of systems may prove most useful in a particular setting. Chances are there is a classification procedure or approach that will fit your needs. In all likelihood, a combination of elements from several systems may be needed to develop the appropriate tool. Existing data or a previously completed classification often will require only minor changes or interpretation to make the information as useful as possible. The following steps are suggested to help you decide on an approach to use for riparian-wetland classification:

- Define your purpose
- Develop a data warehouse
- Develop an understanding of process commensurate with your purpose
- Maintain data integrity

Define Your Purpose

Classification should be a tool that helps you get something done. Classification should not be done for the purpose of classification; it should be based on need. In defining your purpose for classification, you should write a purpose statement that describes exactly what the classification is to provide. It should list management requirements, assumptions, output formats, and goals.

Land Use Planning and Environmental Analysis

Environmental analysis comes from a number of requirements rooted in the National Environmental Policy Act. Analysis can range from project- and site-specific applications, such as environmental assessments (EAs), to broader and programmatic applications, such as resource management plans, to holistic and cumulative applications, such as a watershed analysis. Classification, if well designed, can provide a powerful tool for presenting, describing, and predicting the consequences of management actions.

Environmental analysis requires specialists to describe the riparian and wetland resource as well as to provide some level of prediction of the potential effect of management decisions. Often, the analysis will serve as the basis for more detailed analyses because of specific actions. The importance of structuring the initial classification effort to accommodate future requirements cannot be overemphasized. Classification that simply presents mapping units without some framework for anticipating future management actions may not be very useful.

Proper Functioning Condition Analysis

The BLM has used the PFC analysis since 1993 to provide a barometer of sorts in evaluating the agency's efforts to improve riparian habitat. The PFC analysis involves a qualitative assessment designed to evaluate riparian ecologic and hydrogeomorphic function. It is conducted by a team of specialists who assess 17 items based on a site's perceived potential. Ward et al. (2003) recommended the use of habitat classification and geomorphic classification in combination with PFC to provide the most information about riparian area and stream health.

Resource Restoration, Habitat Creation, and Wetland Mitigation

In recent years, the number of projects related to resource restoration, habitat creation, and wetland mitigation has increased. Classification can provide a useful tool for analyzing conditions and determining restoration, creation, and mitigation goals, priorities, strategies, and design (Sather-Blair et al. 1983, Frissell et al. 1986, Lanka et al. 1987, Delong and Brusven 1991, Moore et al. 1991, Olson and Harris 1997, Harris and Olson 1997, Suzuki and McComb 1998, Wissmar and Beschta 1998, Quinn et al. 2001, and Montgomery 2004). Montgomery (2004), citing Kondolf et al. (2003), suggests that many salmon restoration projects fail because they rely on "off-the-shelf" concepts and designs rather than developing site-specific understanding. He goes on to suggest that salmon recovery efforts, to be successful, need to be rooted in understanding hydrogeomorphic processes and historical changes to rivers and streams. Kondolf (1995) recognized that stream channel classification is commonly carried out by those who are not geomorphologists and who may not fully understand its use. Kondolf et al. (2003) present a discussion on the uses and limitations of such classification tools and document the popularity among land managers of the system developed by Rosgen (1985, 1994). Kondolf (1985) warns, "Despite their real value, classification schemes can be seductive, especially for non-geomorphologists (who are unlikely to appreciate the nature of geomorphological processes), who may feel that the channel is completely described once it has been 'classified.'" Kondolf (1985) also provides an example in which a designer filled a natural pool because it did not fit with the designated stream classification, even though the project was to increase pools in the reach. Fortunately, the trend of classification has been towards developing a better understanding of process. Muller (1997) states, "Classifying riparian vegetation therefore requires a full understanding of species distribution and succession, in relation to environmental parameters and disturbance factors over a large area."

Develop a Data Warehouse

Data warehouse is a term that refers to all of the available data, generally digital, that may be applicable to a project. A typical data set includes historical aerial photographs, oblique photographs, past inventories, maps, and studies. The data may also be useful in determining temporal and spatial changes, cause and effect relationships, and limiting factors.

Riparian inventories have been conducted throughout the West and may be applicable to your need. Look for previous applications of classification in your region and consider using them or their components for your classification project. However, be aware that past classification efforts may not be designed to accommodate your purpose.

Develop an Understanding of Process Commensurate with Your Purpose

Dominant processes, limiting factors, causative and disturbance factors, spatial and temporal factors, and reference areas are all important in understanding how riparian-wetland systems function. A classification that is based on a solid understanding of process can be used to extrapolate cause and effect relationships between similar classification units. A classification that is not based on process will have limited value for extrapolation and can lead to serious judgment errors when used beyond its design. If the purpose of the classification is simply to provide a visual representation of some riparian-wetland characteristic, that fact should be clearly noted in the classification. Classification efforts, particularly those from a decade or more ago, often were used to display meaningful groupings of a resource inventory and nothing more.

In our experience, the most common misapplication of classification information comes from using a dated classification that represents a "snapshot" of resource information where some aspect of the riparian-wetland system has changed. One example is the National Wetland Inventory (NWI). That inventory uses the U.S. Fish and Wildlife Service (USFWS) classification technique developed by Cowardin et al. (1979), which describes the dominant vegetation, and to some degree, expected hydrologic conditions at the time of the inventory. It is an extremely useful technique, but it is not designed nor intended to go much beyond description unless coupled with more process-based analyses. Using NWI information for restoration planning, impact analysis, reference area selection, and other similar applications may be inappropriate, especially where hydrologic or morphologic conditions are complex or variable.

Maintain Data Integrity

Data integrity remains a serious concern when using classification techniques. The actual resource data upon which a classification is based should always be protected and documented. A classification and its data should be permanently joined. Also, a classification technique should help portray the data it is based on and guard against the "point and classify" approach. The "point and classify" approach occurs when an area becomes classified without using data. Sometimes data becomes secondary to classification and users assume that site characteristics of a classified area reflect actual data, which may not be the case. An example of this would be using the Rosgen classification descriptors to describe a riparian-wetland system without actually going through the steps that the classification procedure demands.

IV. Classification Systems and Approaches

This section provides summaries and potential applications for selected classification systems that are useful to riparian and wetland practitioners. They are listed in general hierarchical order: regional systems, geomorphic systems, vegetation systems, and habitat systems. As with any procedure, misapplication is likely to occur if the users rely solely on the classification tool or its products and not on the underlying science behind the classification. Users must always place the science in front of the classification and not the other way around.

Regional Systems

Regional systems are representations of large spatial areas having similar characteristics of broad variables such as climate, geology, soil, vegetation, elevation, or a combination of these variables. Three major regional systems are in wide use: the Natural Resources Conservation Service (NRCS) major land resource area, which is defined in the *National Soil Survey Handbook* (USDA-NRCS 2003), the U.S. Environmental Protection Agency (EPA) ecoregion mapping effort featuring four nested levels of resolution, and the well-known Bailey ecoregion system used by the U.S. Forest Service (USFS) and other groups. These systems are shown in Figure 1a-c.

The usefulness of regional classifications will tie directly to the intended use of the classification

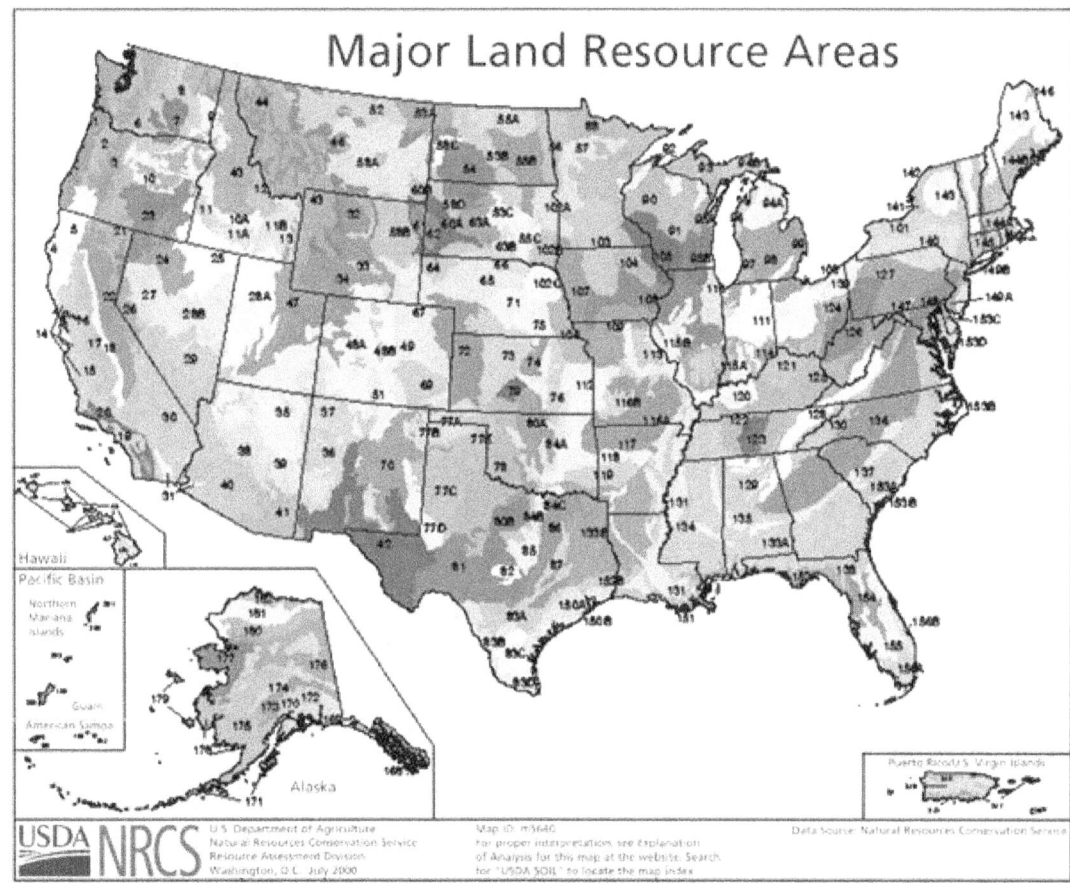

Figure 1a. The major land resource area system is used by the Natural Resources Conservation Service.

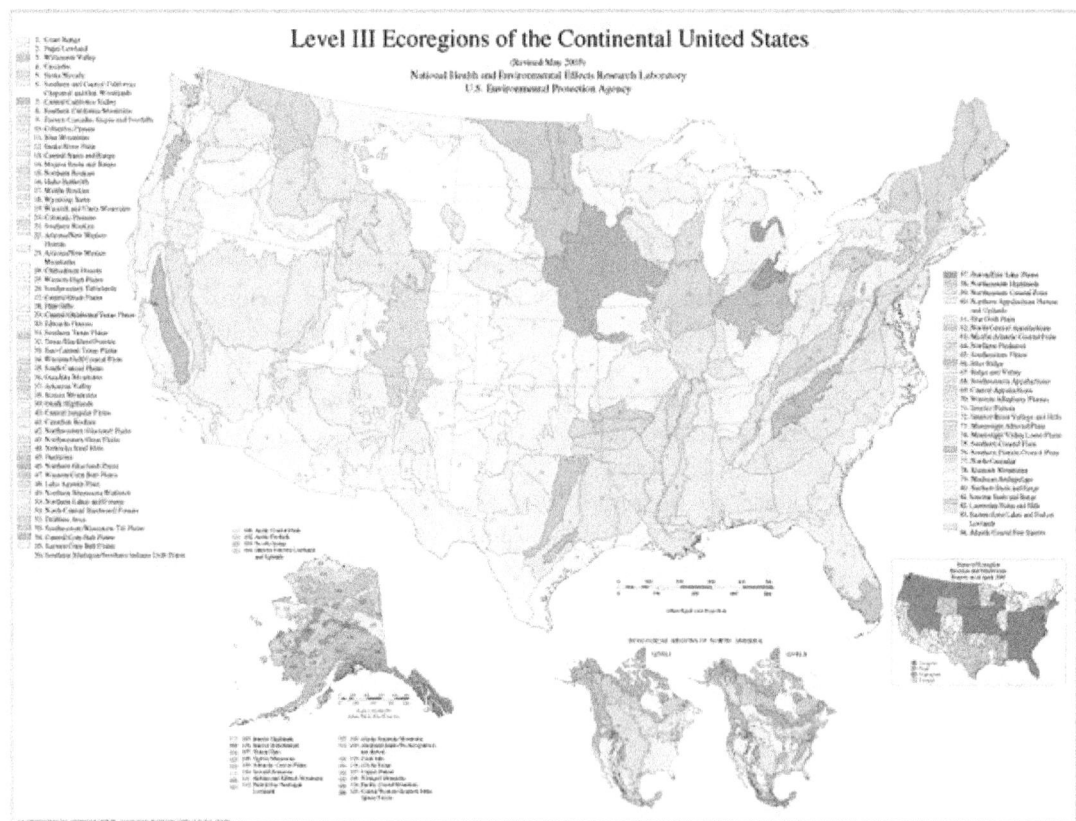

Figure 1b. The ecoregion system used by the Environmental Protection Agency has four levels of resolution.

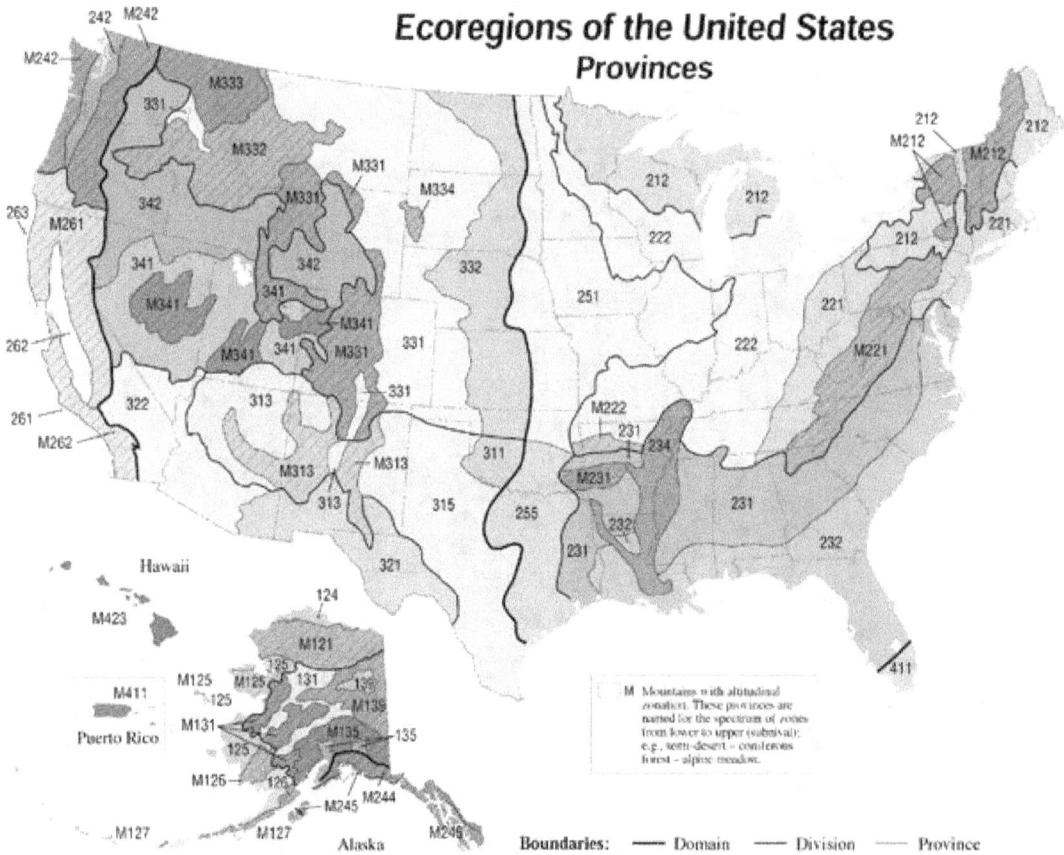

Figure 1c. The Forest Service uses the Bailey (1995) ecoregion system.

project you are embarking on. At a minimum, regional classifications should be examined to:

1. Determine what regional systems are available and used in the project area.
2. Initially identify variability at the regional level within a watershed, which should help to identify important processes.
3. Locate other areas having similar regional classification attributes that can be used for finding potential reference sites and comparable projects and in extrapolating results (Omernik 1995).

Brewer (1999) listed the following factors that guided the development of the EPA ecoregion system:

1. Holistic, broad-based regional analysis and assessment of resource management.
2. Inventory and assessment of environmental resources.
3. Establishment of resource management goals.
4. Wetland classification and management.
5. Development of biological criteria for water quality standards.
6. Refinement of chemical water quality standards.

The above lists should provide suitable ideas for incorporating regional-level classification into more site-specific endeavors.

Major Land Resource Areas

"Major land resource areas (MLRA) are based upon aggregations of geographically associated land resource units and identify nearly homogeneous areas of land use, elevation, topography, climate, water resources, potential natural vegetation, and soils. Major land resource area boundaries reflect an appropriate generalization of land resource unit boundaries (as derived from state soil geographic database map unit boundaries). The approximate minimum size of a major land resource area that may be delineated is 580,644 hectares, or 1,434,803 acres. This minimum delineation is represented at the official major land resource area map scale of 1:7,500,000 by an area approximately 1 cm by 1 cm (0.4 inch by 0.4 inch). Minimum linear delineations are at least 0.3 cm (0.1 inch) in width and 2.5 cm (1 inch) in

length. The Pacific and Caribbean Islands, which have land areas less than 580,644 hectares (1,434,803 acres) in size, are excluded from the minimum delineation rule. Large existing major land resource areas may be subdivided to create more homogeneous areas as needed, provided that cartographic criteria regarding minimum delineations are met. The descriptions of the map units on major land resource area maps emphasize land use and water resource management. Generally, a major land resource area occupies one continuous delineation; but it may occupy several separate ones. Major land resource areas are most useful for statewide agricultural planning and have value for interstate, regional, and national planning" (USDA-NRCS 2003).

Additional information can be found at *http://www.nrcs.usda.gov/technical/land/mlra.*

Ecoregions

"The ecoregion concept, introduced by Crowley (1967), is based on the notion that such homogeneous ecosystem regions exist in nature and can be delineated and classified. This concept is not new, but is merely a new name for old ideas developed in scientific and geographic theory. The ecoregion concept, or theory, is used to create classifications and frameworks that depict ecoregions" (Brewer 1999). Omernik and Bailey (1997) state, "In broad terms, ecological regions, at any scale, can be defined as areas with relative homogeneity in ecosystems."

Additional information can be found at *http://www.epa.gov/wed/pages/ecoregions.htm.*

"Ecoregions denote areas of general similarity in ecosystems and in the type, quality, and quantity of environmental resources. They are designed to serve as a spatial framework for the research, assessment, management, and monitoring of ecosystems and ecosystem components. By recognizing the spatial differences in the capacities and potentials of ecosystems, ecoregions stratify the environment by its probable response to disturbance. These general purpose regions are critical for structuring and implementing ecosystem management strategies across federal agencies, state agencies, and nongovernment organizations that are responsible for different types of resources within the same geographical areas" (Omernik and Bailey 1997).

EPA Ecoregions

Omernik (1995) states "Hence, the difference between this approach to defining ecoregions and most preceding methods is that it is based on the hypothesis that ecological regions gain their identity through spatial differences in a combination of landscape characteristics. The factors that are more or less important vary from one place to another at all scales." Omernik (1995) provides the basis of the EPA methodology that is leading a nationwide effort to provide ecoregion classification at a relatively more detailed, larger scale (level IV), which is available in nearly all of the United States through the cooperation of many federal agencies, including the NRCS and USFS (Figure 2). The assimilation

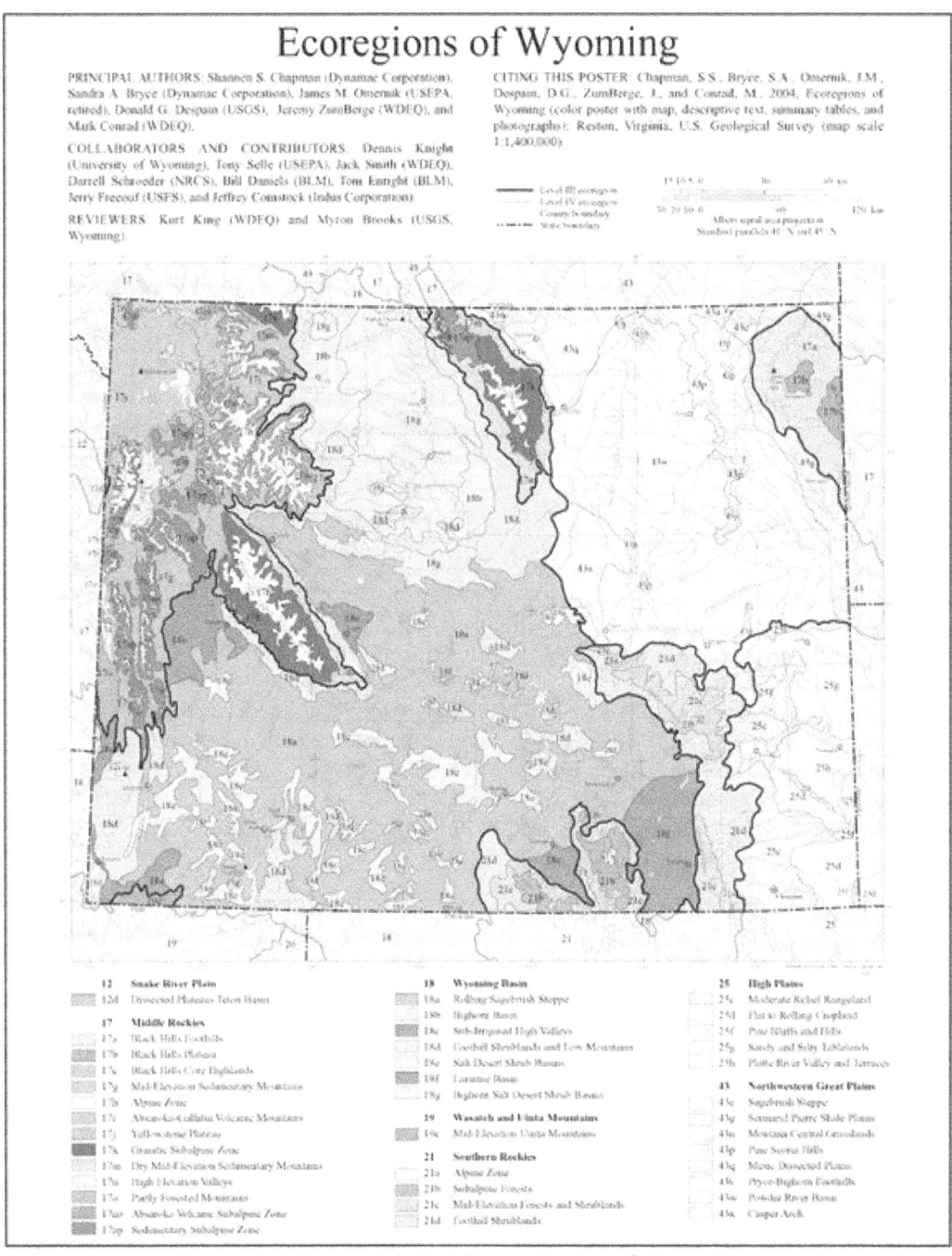

Figure 2. This map of Wyoming illustrates the level IV application of the Environmental Protection Agency's ecoregion system.

of NRCS and USFS regional classifications and state and federal watershed delineation efforts is a credit to those professionals who can see the value of cooperation over competition. The EPA method, while being relatively qualitative, involves local resource experts along with national experts to provide utility and consistency. The qualitative method allows the developers to include features within an ecoregion boundary that might be overlooked in a single-featured classification. At its core, the EPA system's purpose is to provide useful information for managers of water quality and aquatic habitat. As such, the EPA system should provide an excellent information source for riparian and wetland classification efforts.

U.S. Forest Service Ecoregion

The USFS ecoregion effort applies Bailey (1995) and provides an excellent source for classification at the regional level. The following excerpt from Brewer (1999) provides an outstanding review of ecoregion history:

"Robert G. Bailey recognized the need for a comprehensive system for classifying ecosystems to aid regional and national long-range land management and planning. In 1976, Bailey, working for the United States Forest Service, published a map titled 'Ecoregions of the United States,' (Bailey, 1978). This map was published for the Interior Department's Fish and Wildlife Service to aid in the National Wetlands Inventory. In 1978, he published a supplement that contained detailed descriptions of the various ecoregions depicted on the original map.

Bailey's methodology closely paralleled the work of Crowley. He defined ecoregions as geographical zones that represented geographical groups or associations of similarly functioning ecosystems (Bailey, 1983). By analyzing environmental factors that acted as selective forces for the creation of ecosystems, Bailey constructed a 1:7,500,000-scale map of the United States' ecoregions. A detailed explanation of the delineation methods was published in 1983.

Ecoregions, according to Bailey, divided the landscape into variously sized ecosystem units that had significance for development of resources and conservation of the environment. Landscape analysis helped identify ecoregions which were defined as broad areas where one would expect to find similar vegetation and soil associations (Bailey, 1983).

Bailey proposed two important management functions that could be derived from an ecoregion classification. The map suggested the areal extent of productivity relationships derived from experiments and allowed users to apply individual experience. Ecoregion maps also provided a geographical framework that would allow recognition and prediction of similar responses from correspondingly defined sites (Bailey, 1983).

Climate, in Bailey's delineation methodology, became the most important reflection of zonality. Second was surface configuration, or land surface form. Vegetation regions based on Dasman (1969)[1] and Küchler (1973) represented the next level of subdivision. Bailey established a hierarchical order based on sub-continental domains that were defined by broad climatic similarities. The fairly heterogeneous domains could be divided into divisions, which correspond to definite vegetational classifications such as prairies or forests. Zonal soils were given consideration at this level. The next class was the province level, based on climax plant formations. Soil zones also were important for province level delineation. The base level of classification was the section level, based almost entirely on Küchler's potential natural vegetation regions (Bailey, 1983)."

Additional information can be found at *http://www.fs.fed.us/institute/ecolink.html.*

Geomorphic Systems

Riparian and wetland work often involves describing and analyzing stream systems, including the channel, banks, floodplain, terraces, surface and subsurface water, and associated habitats. Several geomorphic systems are now commonly used to classify stream systems. Their basic methodologies and applications are described on the following pages.

---

[1] Complete reference information was not provided in Brewer (1999).

Brinson's Hydrogeomorphic Classification

The hydrogeomorphic (HGM) classification system (Brinson 1993) has been used extensively to better understand and evaluate wetland ecosystems. The HGM procedure emphasizes geomorphic and hydrologic controls, which are most important in defining many riparian and wetland systems. The procedure was designed to be simple to enable fast learning and flexible to allow for revision and correction. Its major purpose is to assess ecosystem function in pre- and postproject situations. HGM can be extremely useful in planning, analysis, and design, as it embraces the concepts of process (function) and reference areas, as well as potential. The procedure is now recommended for developing compensatory mitigation plans (U.S. Army Corps of Engineers 2002), and its expedited development was directed by the White House Office on Environmental Policy in 1993 (Clairain 2002). A vast amount of support literature is available including: a functional assessment of the Upper Yellowstone River (Hauer et al. 2001), functional guidance (Smith et al. 1995, Brinson et al. 1995, Wakely and Smith 2001, Smith and Wakely 2001, and Clairain 2002), a tidal application (Shafer and Yozzo1998), reference area guidance (Smith 2001), prairie pothole guidance (Hauer et al. 2002a), Rocky Mountain riverine floodplains guidance (Hauer et al. 2002b), wetland hydrology guidance (Cole and Wardrop 1997), and impact and mitigation assessments (Hauer and Smith 1998). In addition, the procedure has been evaluated using two support teams on 44 riverine sites demonstrating a high degree of agreement for most variables and Functional Capacity Index scores (Whigham et al. 1999) and the procedure also supports statistical treatment of the scoring within functional category (Pohll et al. 2000).

The HGM procedure uses three components: landscape (geomorphic setting), water source and transport, and hydrodynamics. Geomorphic setting is the wetland's landscape position and is related to how that topographic setting processes water (transport and storage). Examples of geomorphic settings include: areas with no inlet or outlet, streamside zones (riparian), and

shorelines that are associated with depressional, riverine, and fringe wetland classes, respectively. Seven hydrogeomorphic wetland classes currently exist: riverine, depression, slope, organic soil flat, mineral soil flat, estuarine fringe, and lacustrine fringe. The water source for the wetland is generally described as precipitation, groundwater, or surface or near-surface inflow, depending on its importance to the functionality of the wetland. Precipitation would be identified as dominant for bog type wetlands existing in a wet climate, which rarely results in unsaturated conditions. Distinguishing whether a wetland system is from a groundwater or surface water source is more difficult in many cases, but the fundamental determination would be how surface water contributes to the functionality of the wetland. Hydrodynamics refers to the frequency, magnitude, and duration of vertical fluctuations (groundwater and precipitation water sources), unidirectional fluctuations as influenced by surface riverine flooding, and bidirectional fluctuations as seen in wave action and tides in the tidal classes. The following assumptions are inherent in the HGM procedure (Rheinhardt et al. 1997):

1. Ecological processes (functions) in relatively unaltered wetlands occur at levels that are sustainable and predictable for any given HGM wetland type (barring severe natural perturbations).
2. Ecological processes are so similar in form and magnitude within any narrowly defined regional subclass that they shape biotic and abiotic components in ways characteristic for the subclass.
3. Some of these biotic and abiotic parameters can be measured in the field using standard and relatively rapid techniques.
4. Variables derived from field measurement can be combined to coarsely model functions of the subclass.

One of the most useful parts of the HGM procedure is the requirement to link fundamental wetland properties with ecological significance, which results in the identification of wetland function (process). A first step in identifying function is to define reference wetlands, which provide the standard for comparison in the HGM procedure (Clairain 2002). Reference subclass wetlands are assumed to be fully functional and are rated as "1." Other wetlands that are less than fully functional and share the same subclass are rated between "0" and "1." The HGM procedure for riverine systems uses 15 functions distributed among 4 functional areas (Brinson et al. 1995):

Hydrologic
   Dynamic Surface Water Storage
   Long-Term Surface Water Storage
   Energy Dissipation
   Subsurface Storage of Water
   Moderation of Groundwater Flow or Discharge
Biogeochemical
   Nutrient Cycling
   Removal of Imported Elements and Compounds
   Retention of Particulates
   Organic Carbon Export
Plant Habitat
   Maintain Characteristic Plant Communities
   Maintain Characteristic Detrital Biomass
Animal Habitat
   Maintain Spatial Structure of Habitat
   Maintain Interspersion and Connectivity
   Maintain Distribution and Abundance of Invertebrates
   Maintain Distribution and Abundance of Vertebrates

The procedure calls for an application team (A-team) to evaluate functions by further defining them with functional variables, which are the physical process components that enable the function to work. For example, under the "Dynamic Surface Water Storage" function, there are variables such as: *frequency of overbank flow, average depth of inundation, microtopographic complexity, and plant roughness,* which represent the components important to distributing water over the floodplain. Hauer et al. (2002a) defined a surface water function on the Upper Yellowstone River as "Surface Water-Groundwater Storage and Flux" with variables of *frequency of surface flooding, frequency of subsurface flooding, macrotopographic complexity, and geomorphic modification.*

Hauer et al. (2002a) provides an example of the range of functional descriptions for the variable *geomorphic modification:*

Description	Score
No geomorphic modifications (e.g., dikes, levees, riprap, bridge approaches, roadbeds, etc.) made to contemporary (Holocene) floodplain surface.	1.0
Few changes to the floodplain surface with little impact on flooding. Changes restricted to < 1m in elevation and only for farm roads or bridges with culverts maintained. Geomorphic modifications do, however, result in minor change in cut-and-fill alluviation.	0.75
Modification to the floodplain surface <1 m in elevation. Riverbank with control structures (e.g., riprap) <10% of river length along LAA [landscape assessment area]. Geomorphic modifications result in measurable change in cut-and-fill alluviation.	0.5
Multiple geomorphic modifications to the floodplain surface to control flood energy, often with bank control structures, but still permitting flow access via culverts to backwater and side channels. Geomorphic modifications result in significant reduction in cut-and-fill alluviation.	0.25
Complete geomorphic modification along the river channel of the floodplain surface to control flood energy. Bank control structures in the form of dikes and riprap in a continuous structure or constructed to prevent channel avulsion, but still permitting flow access via culverts to backwater and side channels. Geomorphic modifications result in termination of cut-and-fill alluviation.	0.1
Complete geomorphic modification along the river channel of the floodplain surface to control flood energy. Bank control structures in the form of dikes and riprap in a continuous structure preventing channel avulsion and also preventing flow access via culverts to backwater and side channels	0

These types of descriptions provide excellent documentation that is useful in analyzing impacts, developing design goals for restoration activities, and establishing action levels for monitoring plans.

The HGM procedure results in the development of regional standards for wetland functions, particularly in assessing mitigation, enhancement, and creation of wetland in a regulatory setting, which was a primary purpose for its development. The full application and accounting of wetland functions can be arduous to those developing the standards (akin to the habitat evaluation procedure), but can be well worth the investment in providing a rapid comparison technique that is process based and well-documented. The HGM procedural concept also can be used in a less intensive manner to fit many BLM needs, such as in environmental analysis and planning, ecosystem analysis, and watershed analysis, and as a companion in conducting the proper functioning condition assessments. The thought process used in the HGM procedure serves as a technical framework that can lead to process-based analysis.

The HGM procedure does not determine value, is not intended for comparing different subclasses, and is not intended for analyzing cumulative impacts (Clairain 2002). Value is defined as "the rules that determine what people consider important" (Brinson 1993). In the process of identifying wetland and riparian units, their functional importance may provide an opportunity to assign or describe their value as it relates to the ecosystem. Certainly determining their monetary value is another exercise. Hauer et al. (2001) demonstrated the use of the HGM procedure in a cumulative impact analysis of the Upper Yellowstone River. Using HGM and other impact assessment procedures, they produced a suitable impact analysis for the wetland ecosystem.

As with any procedure, misapplication is likely to occur if the users rely solely on the classification tool or its products, such as on HGM models, and not on the underlying science behind the classification. Users must always place the science in front of the classification and not the other way around.

Rosgen's Classification of Natural Rivers

Rosgen's (1994, 1996) classification of natural rivers is designed to:

- Predict a river's behavior from its appearance
- Develop specific hydraulic and sediment relations for a given morphological channel type and state
- Provide a mechanism to extrapolate site-specific data collected on a given stream reach to those of similar character
- Provide a consistent and reproducible frame of reference of communication for those working with river systems in a variety of professional disciplines.

Rosgen (1994) acknowledges the complexity of natural rivers and states, "Obviously, a classification scheme risks over-simplification of a very complex system." With this in mind, Rosgen (1996) suggests that "stream morphology displays a continuum of form" and develops a stream classification system progressing through four hierarchical levels: a broad geomorphic assessment (level I); a more detailed description based on reference reach information (level II); a description of existing condition (level III); and, finally, verification where measurements are made to determine the strength of process assumptions used in the previous levels (level IV).

Level I begins with characterizing the basin's landform and valley types and integrating this information with observed stream morphology based on form and pattern. A characteristic "stream type" is determined from parameters of entrenchment, pattern, slope, and channel shape to be one of nine types (Aa+, A, B, C, D, DA, E, F, and G). The level I classification strives to provide a consistent initial framework for organizing information and communication. In addition, this level helps to develop priorities and consider other resource inventories that share the stream system.

Level II stream types develop more refinement using field measurements to help resolve questions regarding sediment supply, sensitivity to disturbance, resiliency, channel response, and habitat potential. The level II step assumes, as does the remainder of the hierarchy, that the stream system behaves as a continuum. At the level II step, because of its relationship with width and channel patterns, bankfull discharge becomes the most important characteristic in the classification system and is required in estimating two of the five level II criteria. The application of the level II stream type results in the refinement of the level I determination, for example, from a "C" type to "C3" and "C4" types. Unfortunately, in our experience, many users of the Rosgen system stop at the level II step.

The level III step provides some of the most useful information about stream behavior and management and requires the user to figure out what the stream is doing and what it has done. Level III involves collecting and analyzing data about vegetation, streamflow, stream size and order, debris and blockages, depositional patterns, meander patterns, streambank erosion potential, aggradation or degradation potential, channel stability, and altered channel materials and dimensions. At this level, the user is asked to develop a description of the "full operating potential" for a particular reach, along with its departure. This step is demanding and requires a high degree of experience not generally available to those who are not geomorphologists, but it can provide valuable information for resource management.

Level IV requires a stream inventory to validate the predictions made in level III. The inventory techniques are selected to compare a reach of interest to some reference or baseline. Techniques may include such things as vertical stability, lateral stability, and bed material. The inherent variability among these types of parameters may require exceptional sampling design or long periods of time for validation.

Some geomorphologists (Juracek and Fitzpatrick 2003, Kondolf et al. 2003, and Miller and Ritter 1996) advise caution to those considering using the Rosgen system for other than descriptive purposes, such as for stream rehabilitation, restoration, or creation. Users should be aware of the data required by the methodology and avoid overextension or misapplication. A number of authors have found Rosgen's system useful for descriptive and habitat application purposes (Tsao et al. 1996, Savery et al. 2001, FISRWG 1998).

Montgomery and Buffington's Stream Classification

Montgomery and Buffington (1993) proposed a classification primarily for streams in the Pacific Northwest. The hierarchy of classification is based on a range of rivers that are sediment limited to transport limited and placed into bedrock, alluvial, and colluvial groups, respectively. Stream groups include colluvial, bedrock, cascade, step-pool, plane-bed, pool-riffle, regime, and braided. River characteristics such as bed material, pattern, transport/depositional reach, dominant roughness features, dominant sediment sources, dominant sediment storage features, slope, confinement, and pool spacing are used in the classification. The strength of this system is in its simplicity and descriptive names. A system of this type is conducive to habitat management and hierarchical integration with other classifications such as habitat types for fish.

Other Geomorphic Classification Systems

Many other river and stream classifications are available. Kondolf et al. (2003) provides an excellent review of river classification, which includes the history, application, evolution, and a brief description of several dozen systems.

Vegetation Systems

Wetland Classification

Classification of Wetlands and Deepwater Habitats of the United States (Cowardin et al. 1979) is the basis for the USFWS National Wetlands Inventory and is a major reference for many wetland regulatory guidance documents. The classification is designed for new inventories of wetlands and deepwater habitats and is intended to describe ecological taxa, arrange them in a system useful to resource managers, furnish units for mapping, and provide uniformity of concepts and terms. The principal users for this classification system are land managers and biologists. The system provides hierarchical levels from the broad functional level (marine, estuarine, riverine, lacustrine, palustrine) to a habitat-level dominance type, which is named for the dominant plant or animal form of the area. The hierarchical structure is provided below:

Classification Units	Description
System	Basic water source/feature (marine, estuarine, riverine, etc.).
Subsystem	Basic water persistence attributes (subtidal, intertidal, lower perennial, upper perennial, etc.).
Class	Gross substrate/vegetation form (rock bottom, aquatic bed, emergent wetland, rocky shore, forested wetland, etc.).
Subclass	Specific substrate/vegetation type (bedrock, sand, mud, needle-leaved evergreen, broad-leaved deciduous, etc.).
Dominance Type	Dominant plant/animal species (horsetail, black cottonwood, willow, caddisfly, crayfish, etc.).
Modifiers	Site-specific attributes of soil, regime, water chemistry, and land alteration (salinity, pH, flooding condition, mineral or organic, farmed, diked, etc.).

This system is currently used by many agencies, organizations, and individuals for the general inventory and classification of habitats. It has been used in small and large applications. Products from the classification can give managers a good overview of the resource. The system is easy to apply and particularly useful with aerial photos. However, it becomes more complex as modifiers, such as specific hydrology and water chemistry modifiers, are added to the description. The addition of modifiers changes this procedure from a wetland and riparian vegetation classification procedure to one that is more process-based, since determining water regime, chemistry, alteration, and certain other characteristics requires some thought on how the wetland functions. This procedure can be used to describe the state of a riparian system, but not the cause and effect relationships that would be useful in determining potential state changes in a riparian system.

The USFWS is open to incorporating more detailed modifiers, such as soils information. Standard soil taxonomic classification can

be placed into the procedure at the modifier level. The dominance level is fairly standard as vegetation descriptions go. Some differences between other procedures can be expected in the delineation between overstory, dominance density, etc. The procedure also appears to fit into other vegetation classification schemes, such as those used on a regional or provincial level. Overall, the procedure recognizes the difference between fluvial surfaces and major vegetation forms at a level that makes it reasonably easy to merge with classification procedures for other considerations, such as geology, climate, and landforms.

Because of its relative simplicity, the USFWS procedure has become an ideal tool for the initial inventory of the nation's wetlands. Most wetlands in the United States are currently mapped and available in digital format. The procedure was not designed to reflect potential natural communities or community ecology. However, additional classification using some of the successional procedures discussed could provide such information within the mapping boundaries of the existing wetland areas.

Successional Classification

Currently, the most frequently used procedure for classifying community ecology follows the concepts introduced by Daubenmire (1959). Many investigators have used these concepts in their work with riparian and wetland environments (Youngblood et al. 1985, Kovalchik 1987, Hansen et al. 1988, Hansen 1989, Szaro 1989, and Hansen et al. 1995). These authors demonstrate that the concepts of succession used in upland environments are equally applicable to riparian systems, although riparian sites are generally much more dynamic. A review and comparison of some of the basic terminology and concepts applied in these documents follows:

- **Association**—In normal usage, an association is a climax community type or potential plant community. In riparian systems, because of their dynamic nature, a true climax community may not have an opportunity to occur (Youngblood et al. 1985). An association for a riparian environment is therefore a plant community type representing the latest successional stage attainable on a specific hydrologically influenced surface (Kovalchik 1987, Hansen 1989). Hansen (1989) uses the term "riparian association," while Youngblood et al. (1985) chose the term "potential stable community type" that approaches an association.

- **Community Type**—This is defined as an aggregation of all plant communities in some procedures or as existing or dominant plant communities in others. Community types are distinguished by floristic and structural similarities in both overstory and undergrowth layers. Community types are considered to represent seral stages.

- **Site Type**—This is the area of land occupied or potentially occupied by a specific association. Site types that are the same would have similar environments that could develop the same potential plant community. Hansen (1989) uses the term "riparian site type" when describing a site capable of producing a "riparian association."

Standard Ecological Site Description Classification

The NRCS *National Range Handbook* (USDA-SCS 1976), as supplemented by the BLM *National Range Handbook* (H-4410-1) (USDI-BLM 1990), includes procedures for preparing standardized ecological site (range site) descriptions. The NRCS handbook provides for range site descriptions that include a unique name, physiographic features, climatic features, vegetation ecology and production, soils, and management interpretations (which can be used in making management recommendations). Early in 1988, BLM determined that the standard site description procedures as applied to uplands would accommodate land features associated with riparian and wetland sites as well. The BLM handbook further applies the procedure to grazable woodlands, forests, and riparian and wetland sites.

The standard ecological site description procedure is for all levels of land users and is applicable to rangeland, woodland, and native pasture. The system is hierarchical, using classification units of physiographic regions, climatic features, vegetation ecology, soils, associated water features, and the primary unit, site. An identifier is also used, which is a reference to a major land resource area, similar to a regional ecological setting. A major purpose of the procedure is to define community response and the reasons why a particular response occurs. The procedure is well suited for identifying changes of state and the reasons for site progression (aggradation/degradation). Use of this procedure is limited by the extent of knowledge of similar sites and by the expertise of the users. Experienced personnel are required to correctly identify site potential. The end product of the procedure is a very useful document for management. The procedure makes use of other nationally or internationally recognized procedures, such as those in the *National Soil Survey Handbook* (USDA-NRCS 2003). It is conceptually similar to others in recognizing a potential or climax plant community and successional stages or communities. The procedure in the *National Range Handbook* (USDA-SCS 1976) is used worldwide to prepare site descriptions for rangelands. These procedures have been modified, tested, and validated for use in preparing site descriptions for riparian areas. Procedures for site correlation exist and are compatible with the *National Soil Survey Handbook* (USDA-NRCS 2003).

The ease of the application of this procedure depends on the ability and experience of the users. A team of specialists, consisting of a biologist, botanist or ecologist, soil scientist, and hydrologist, is required to use these procedures on riparian and wetland sites. The procedures for mapping, delineating, describing, and interpreting sites have been used by several agencies for several years. Sufficient training, review, and correlation are key to the success of the procedure.

Habitat Systems

Habitat level classifications are used to provide information for discrete and small features within a riparian system at a large scale. These classifications are often specialized, looking for particular habitat structures and characteristics that are important to specific species. Examples would include classification for beaver habitat (Suzuki and McComb 1998), vegetation used by particular songbirds, and fish habitat. Probably the best known habitat classification system involves the channel geomorphic unit (American Fisheries Society 1999), based on Bisson et al. (1982) and later refined by Hawkins et al. (1993).

V. Conclusion

Riparian-wetland resource data spans a number of disciplines, as illustrated in the previous descriptions of classification tools. Riparian-wetland management has become much more complex in recent years, concerned with not only vegetation, fisheries, water quality, geomorphology, or wildlife but with all of these characteristics. The assessment of the riparian-wetland resource is typically a team effort now, with several disciplines working together to design inventories and collect, analyze, interpret, and present data to develop a product that is most useful for resource management.

The classification systems presented in this document can be combined to produce very powerful presentation and assessment products.

Coupled with advanced inventory design and geographic information systems, the appropriate classification systems can be integrated to solve many problems. Approaches that integrate process-based hydrogeomorphological classification as a basic structure will benefit from an increased ability to extrapolate information and make better resource decisions.

Riparian-wetland systems are dynamic, for the most part, and therefore require the information base used to manage them to be dynamic as well. Classification techniques and the data they are built upon should be routinely and systematically updated to keep pace with changes not only in the riparian-wetland systems, but also in our understanding of the science pertaining to them.

References Cited

American Fisheries Society. 1999. Aquatic habitat assessment: Common methods. Edited by M.B. Bain and N.J. Stevenson. American Fisheries Society, Bethesda, MD. 8 pp.

Bailey, R.G. 1978. Description of the ecoregions of the United States. USDA Forest Service, Intermtn. Reg. Ogden, UT. 76 pp.

Bailey, R.G. 1983. Delineation of ecosystem regions. Environmental Management. 7(4): 365-73.

Bailey, R.G. 1995. Description of the ecoregions of the United States (2nd edition). Misc. Pub. No. 1391, map scale 1:7,500,000. USDA Forest Service. 108 pp.

Bisson, P.S., J.L. Nielsen, R.A. Palmason, and L.E. Grove. 1982. A system of naming habitat types in small streams, with examples of habitat utilization by salmonids during low streamflow. *In:* Acquisition and utilization of aquatic habitat inventory information. Edited by N.G. Armantrout. American Fisheries Society, Bethesda, MD. pp. 62-73.

Brewer, I. 1999. The conceptual development and use of ecoregion classifications. Unpublished thesis, Oregon State University. Online at ***www.cartographica.com/Ecoregions.htm***. Accessed on 6/24/2005.

Brinson, M.M. 1993. A hydrogeomorphic classification for wetlands. Wetlands Research Program Technical Report WRP-DE-4. U.S. Army Corps of Engineers, Vicksburg, MS. 103 pp.

Brinson, M.M., F.R. Hauer, L.C. Lee, W.L. Nutter, R.D. Rheinhardt, R.D. Smith, and D. Whigham. 1995. A guidebook for application of hydrogeomorphic assessments to riverine wetlands. Technical Report WRP-DE-11. NTIS No. AD A308 365. U.S. Army Engineer Waterways Experiment Station, Vicksburg, MS. 219 pp.

Clairain, E.J. 2002. Hydrogeomorphic approach to assessing wetland functions: Guidelines for developing regional guidebooks: Chapter 1—Introduction and overview of the hydrogeomorphic approach. ERDC/EL TR-02-3. U.S. Army Engineer Research and Development Center, Vicksburg, MS. 39 pp.

Cole, C.A. and D.H. Wardrop. 1997. Wetland hydrology as a function of hydrogeomorphic (HGM) subclass. Wetlands (17):4 456-467.

Cowardin L.M., V. Carter, F. Golet, and E. LaRoe. 1979. Classification of wetlands and deepwater habitats of the United States. FWS/OBS-79/31. U.S. Department of the Interior, Fish and Wildlife Service, Washington, DC. 103 pp.

Crowley, J.M. 1967. Biogeography. Canadian Geographer: 11(4):312-26.

Daubenmire, R.D. 1959. A canopy-covered method of vegetation analysis. Northwest Science 33:43-66.

Delong, M.D. and M.A. Brusven. 1991. Classification and spatial mapping of riparian habitat with applications toward management of streams impacted by nonpoint source pollution. Env. Mgt. 15(4):565-571.

FISWG. 1998. Stream corridor restoration: Principles, processes, and practices. Federal Interagency Stream Restoration Working Group (15 Federal agencies). GPO Item No. 0120-A. Superintendent of Documents No. A 57.6/2:EN 3/PT.653. ISBN-0-934213-59-3.

Frissell, C.A., W.J. Liss, C.E. Warren, and M.D. Hurley. 1986. A hierarchical framework for stream habitat classification: Viewing streams in a watershed context. Environmental Management, 10:199–214.

Gurnell, A.M., P. Angold, and K.J. Gregory. 1994. Classification of river corridors: Issues to be addressed in developing an operational methodology. Aquatic Conserv: Mar. Freshw. Ecosyst. 4:219–231.

Hansen, P. 1989. Inventory, classification, and management of riparian sites along the upper Missouri national wild and scenic river. Montana Riparian Association, School of Forestry, University of Montana. 213 pp.

Hansen, P., S.W. Chadde, R. Pfister. 1988. Riparian dominance types of Montana. Misc. Publ. No. 49. Montana Forest and Conservation Experiment Station, School of Forestry, University of Montana, Missoula, MT. 411 pp.

Hansen, P.L., R.D. Pfister, K. Boggs, B.J. Cook, J. Joy, and D.K. Hinckley. 1995. Classification and management of Montana's riparian and wetland sites. Misc. Publication No. 54. School of Forestry, University of Montana, Missoula, MT.

Harris, R. and C. Olson. 1997. Two-stage system for prioritizing riparian restoration at the stream reach and community scales. Restoration Ecology 5(4S):34-42.

Hauer, F.R. and R.D. Smith. 1998. The hydrogeomorphic approach to functional assessment of riparian wetlands: Evaluating impacts and mitigation on river floodplains in the U.S.A. Freshwater Biology 40:517-530.

Hauer, F.R., B.J. Cook, M. Miller, C. Noble, and T. Gonser. 2001. Upper Yellowstone River Hydrogeomorphic Functional Assessment for Temporal and Synoptic Cumulative Impact Analyses. ERDC TN-WRAP-01-03. U.S. Army Research and Development Center, Vicksburg, MS.

Hauer, F.R., B.J. Cook, M.C. Gilbert, E.J. Clairain, and R.D. Smith. 2002a. A regional guidebook for applying the hydrogeomorphic approach to assessing wetland functions of intermontane prairie pothole wetlands in the northern Rocky Mountains. ERDC/EL TR-02-7. U.S. Army Engineer Research and Development Center, Vicksburg, MS.

Hauer, F.R., B.J. Cook, M.C. Gilbert, E.J. Clairain, and R.D. Smith. 2002b. A regional guidebook for applying the hydrogeomorphic approach to assessing wetland functions of riverine floodplains in the northern Rocky Mountains. ERDC/EL TR-02-21. U.S. Army Engineer Research and Development Center, Vicksburg, MS.

Hawkins, C.P., J.L. Kershner, P.A. Bisson, M.D. Bryant, L.M. Decker, S.V. Gregory, D.A. McCullough, C.K. Overton, G.H. Reeves, R.J. Steedman, and M.K. Young. 1993. A hierarchical approach to classifying stream habitat features. Fisheries 18(6):3-12.

Heritage, G.L., M.E. Charlton, and S. O'Regan. 2001. Morphological classification of fluvial environments: An investigation of the continuum of channel types. Journal of Geology 109:21-33.

Juracek, K.E. and F.A. Fitzpatrick. 2003. Limitations and implications of stream classification. Journal of the American Water Resources Association 69(3):659-670.

Kondolf, G.M. 1995. Geomorphological stream channel classification in aquatic habitat restoration: uses and limitations. Aquatic Conservation: Marine and Freshwater Ecosystems 5:127-141.

Kondolf, G.M., D.R. Montgomery, H. Piegay, L. Schmitt. 2003. Geomorphic classification of rivers and streams. *In:* Tools in fluvial geomorphology. Edited by G.M. Kondolf and H. Piegay. John Wiley & Sons, Chichester. pp. 171-204.

Kovalchik, B.L. 1987. Riparian zone associations: Deschutes, Ochoco, Fremont, and Winema National Forests. USDA Forest Service Region 6 Ecology Technical Paper 29-87. Pacific Northwest Region, Portland, OR. 171 pp.

Kovalchik, B.L. and L.A. Chitwood. 1990. Use of geomorphology in the classification of riparian plant associations in mountainous landscapes of central Oregon, U.S.A. Forest Ecology and Management 33/34 405-418.

Küchler, A.W. 1973. Problems in classifying and mapping vegetation for ecological regionalization. Ecology 54:512-23.

Lanka, R.P., W.A. Hubert, and T.A. Wesche. 1987. Relations of geomorphology to stream habitat and trout standing stock in small Rocky Mountain streams. Trans. Am. Fish. Soc. 116:21-28.

Miller, J.R. and J.B. Ritter. 1996. Discussion: An examination of the Rosgen classification of natural rivers. Catena 27:295-299.

Montgomery, D.R. 2004. Geology, geomorphology, and the restoration ecology of salmon. GSA Today 14(11):4-12.

Montgomery, D.R. and J.M. Buffington. 1993. Channel classification, prediction of channel response and assessment of channel condition. Report TFW-SH10-93-002. Department of Geological Sciences and Quaternary Research Center, University of Washington, Seattle.

Moore, T., R.C. Ford, and M.G. Parsons. 1991. Use of a habitat-based stream classification system for categorizing trout biomass. North American Journal of Fisheries Management 11:305-311.

Mosely, M.P. 1987. The classification and characterization of rivers. In River channels environment and process. Edited by K. Richards. Oxford, Blackwell, pp. 295-320.

Muller, E. 1997. Mapping riparian vegetation along rivers: Old concepts and new methods. Aquatic Botany 58:411-437.

Olson, C. and R. Harris. 1997. Applying a two-stage system to prioritize riparian restoration at the San Luis Rey River, San Diego County, California. Restoration Ecology 5(4S):43-55.

Omernik, J.M. 1995. Ecoregions: A framework for managing ecosystems. The George Wright Forum 12(1):35-50.

Omernik, J.M. 2003. The misuse of hydrologic unit maps for extrapolation, reporting, and ecosystem management. J. Am. Water Resources Assn. 39(3):563-573.

Omernik, J.M. and R.G. Bailey. 1997. Distinguishing between watersheds and ecoregions. Journal of the American Water Resources Association 33(5):935-949.

Pohll, G., J. Tracy, and R. Smith. 2000. Numerical assessment of hydrogeomorphic wetland functions. In: Wetlands and remediation—An international conference—Salt Lake City, 1999. Edited by J.L. Means and R.E. Hinchee. Battelle Press, Columbus, Ohio.

Quinn, J.M., P.M. Brown, W. Boyce, S. Mackay, A. Taylor, and T. Fenton. 2001. Riparian zone classification for management of stream water quality and ecosystem health. J. Amer. Wat. Res. Assoc. 37(6):1509-1515.

Rheinhardt, R.D., M.M. Brinson, and P.M. Farley. 1997. Applying wetland reference data to functional assessment, mitigation, and restoration. Wetlands 17:2 195-215.

Rosgen, D.L. 1985. A stream classification system. Presented at the Symposium on Riparian Ecosystems and Their Management: Reconciling Conflicting Uses. April 16-18, Tucson, AZ.

Rosgen, D. 1994. A classification of natural rivers. Catena 22:160-199.

Rosgen D. 1996. Applied river morphology. Wildland Hydrology. Pagosa Springs, CO. 363 pp.

Sather-Blair, S., C.L. Blair, K. Gebhardt, J. Gebhardt, H. Harper, J. Mills, and A. Thomas. 1983. Boise River wildlife and fish habitat study—Wetland inventory and management guidelines. Resource Systems, Inc., Boise, Idaho.

Savery, T.S., G.H. Belt, and D. Higgens. 2001. Evaluation of the Rosgen stream classification system in Chequamegon-Nicolet National Forest, Wisconsin. J. AWRA. 37:3 (641-654).

Shafer, D.J. and D.J. Yozzo. 1998. National guidebook for application of hydrogeomorphic assessment of tidal fringe wetlands. Technical Report WRP-DE-16. U.S. Army Engineer Waterways Experiment Station, Vicksburg, MS.

Smith, R.D. 2001. Hydrogeomorphic approach to assessing wetland functions: Guidelines for developing regional guidebooks: Chapter 3—Developing a reference wetland system. ERDC/EL TR-01-29. U.S. Army Engineer Research and Development Center, Vicksburg, MS.

Smith, R.D., A. Ammann, C. Bartoldus, and M.M. Brinson. 1995. An approach for assessing wetland functions using hydrogeomorphic classification, reference wetlands, and functional indices. Technical Report WRP-DE-9. NTIS No. AD A307 121. U.S. Army Engineer Waterways Experiment Station, Vicksburg, MS.

Smith, R.D. and J.S. Wakeley. 2001. Hydrogeomorphic approach to assessing wetland functions: Guidelines for developing regional guidebooks: Chapter 4—Developing assessment models. ERDC/EL TR-01-30. U.S. Army Engineer Research and Development Center, Vicksburg, MS.

Suzuki, N. and W.C. McComb. 1998. Habitat classification models for beaver (castor canadensis) in the streams of the central Oregon Coast Range. Northwest Science 72(2):102-110.

Szaro, R.C. 1989. Riparian forest and scrubland community types of Arizona and New Mexico. Desert Plant 9:3-4(70-138).

Thomson, J.R., M.P. Taylor, and G.J. Brierley. 2004. Are river styles ecologically meaningful? A test of the ecological significance of a geomorphic river characterization scheme. Aquatic Conserv: Mar. Freshw. Ecosyst. 14:25–48.

Tsao, E.H, L. Lin, E.P. Bergersen, R. Behnke, and C. Chiou. 1996. A stream classification system for identifying reintroduction sites of Formosan landlocked salmon. Acta Zoologica Taiwanica 7(1):39-59.

U.S. Army Corps of Engineers. 2002. Regulatory Guidance Letter 02-2. Washington, DC.

U.S. Department of Agriculture, Natural Resources Conservation Service. 2003. National soil survey handbook, title 430-VI. Online at *http://soils.usda.gov/technical/handbook/*. Accessed on July 12, 2005.

U.S. Department of Agriculture, Soil Conservation Service. 1976. National range handbook, as amended. Washington, DC. 143 pp.

U.S. Department of the Interior. 1990. National range handbook. BLM Manual Handbook H-4410-1. Bureau of Land Management, Washington, DC.

Van Deusen, R.D. 1954. Maryland freshwater stream classification by watersheds. Chesapeake Biol. Lab. 106:1-30.

Wakeley, J.S. and R.D. Smith. 2001. Hydrogeomorphic approach to assessing wetland functions: Guidelines for developing regional guidebooks: Chapter 7—Verifying, field testing, and validating assessment models. ERDC/EL TR-01-31. U.S. Army Engineer Research and Development Center, Vicksburg, MS.

Ward, T.A., K.W. Tate, E.R. Atwill, D.F. Lile, D.L. Lancaster, N. McDougald, S. Barry, R.S. Ingram, H.A. George, W. Jensen, W.E. Frost, R. Phillips, G.G. Markegard, and S. Larson. 2003. A comparison of three visual assessments for riparian and stream health. Journal of Soil and Water Conservation 58(2): 83-88.

Whigham, D.F., L.C. Lee, M.M. Brinson, R.D. Rheinhardt, M.C. Rains, J.A. Mason, H. Kahn, M.B. Ruhlman, and W.L. Nutter. 1999. Hydrogeomorphic (HGM) assessment—A test of user consistency. Wetlands 19:3 560-569.

Wissmar, R.C. and R.L. Beschta. 1998. Restoration and management of riparian ecosystems: A catchment perspective. Freshwater Biology 40:571-585.

Youngblood, A.P., W.G. Padgett, and A.H. Winward. 1985. Riparian community type classification of eastern Idaho-western Wyoming. USDA Forest Service, Intermountain Region, R4-Ecol-85-01. 78 pp.